Shining Star

A Kid's Guide to an Awesome Christian Life

Leah Katerberg

Doing life with God
...your adventure begins!
Leah

WestBow Press books may be ordered through booksellers or by contacting:

WestBow Press
A Division of Thomas Nelson & Zondervan
1663 Liberty Drive
Bloomington, IN 47403
www.westbowpress.com
1 (866) 928-1240

Because of the dynamic nature of the Internet, any web addresses or links contained in this book may have changed since publication and may no longer be valid. The views expressed in this work are solely those of the author and do not necessarily reflect the views of the publisher, and the publisher hereby disclaims any responsibility for them.

Any people depicted in stock imagery provided by Thinkstock are models, and such images are being used for illustrative purposes only. Certain stock imagery © Thinkstock.

ISBN: 978-1-4908-1519-0 (sc)
ISBN: 978-1-4908-1520-6 (e)

Library of Congress Control Number: 2013919951

Printed in the United States of America.

WestBow Press rev. date: 7/29/2014

Scripture taken from the Common English Bible®, CEB® Copyright © 2010, 2011 by Common English Bible.™ Used by permission. All rights reserved worldwide. The "CEB" and "Common English Bible" trademarks are registered in the United States Patent and Trademark Office by Common English Bible. Use of either trademark requires the permission of Common English Bible.

Scriptures taken from the Holy Bible, New International Version®, NIV®. Copyright © 1973, 1978, 1984, 2011 by Biblica, Inc.™ Used by permission of Zondervan. All rights reserved worldwide. www.zondervan.com The "NIV" and "New International Version" are trademarks registered in the United States Patent and Trademark Office by Biblica, Inc.™ All rights reserved.

WESTBOW®
PRESS
A DIVISION OF THOMAS NELSON
& ZONDERVAN

List of Chapters

Before You Start Reading this Book...

If you know God, your life looks different than if you didn't. It is a life that you are excited about living, a life that others see and want to follow.

The Bible tells us that Christians are like Shining Stars, giving light for everyone to see who God is and why his way is the best way to live.

This book shows 12 important things to help you be a Shining Star. You might want to read one each day, or one each week, or even read the whole book at once. However you decide to read it, it's a good idea to talk to other Christians (maybe a parent or Sunday school teacher) about what you're reading so that they can help you understand the things you're learning.

Your life is a non-stop adventure as you learn more about God and live with Him and for Him. You will shine brighter and brighter each day!

Among these people you shine like stars in the world because you hold on to the word of life.
Philippians 2:15-16 (Common English Bible)

Verses from the Bible about Each Chapter

1. Shining Stars See the Big Picture
Luke 12:7, Psalm 147:5, Isaiah 40:28, Jeremiah 29:11, Matthew 5:14-16, 1 John 4:12

2. Shining Stars Focus on God, Not on Rules
Ephesians 2:8-10, Romans 4:4-5, Hebrews 4:16, Romans 5:8, Psalm 147:10-11, Romans 11:6

3. Shining Stars Think God is Amazing
See verses listed in chapter

4. Shining Stars Know Why Jesus Lived, Died, and Lived Again
Mark 14-16, John 3:16, John 14:6, John 10:30, 1 Timothy 3:16, Matthew 28:18-20

5. Shining Stars Listen to God's Spirit
John 16:12-15, John 14:16-17, John 14:25-26, 2 Corinthians 3:17, 2 Timothy 3:15-17, John 10:27, Revelation 3:20, Hebrews 4:12

6. Shining Stars Talk with God
Mark 1:35-37, Luke 6:12-13, Luke 5:15-16, Matthew 6:5-13, 1 John 5:14-15, Colossians 1:9-12, Matthew 6:31-32, John 5:19, John 8:26, Romans 8:26

7. Shining Stars Thank God for Taking Care of Them
Matthew 6:25-34, 1 Timothy 6:7-8, Ephesians 5:20, 1 Thessalonians 5:16-18, Psalm 106:1, Philippians 4:6,19, Colossians 4:2, Hebrews 13:5, Proverbs 17:22

8. Shining Stars Let God's Flashlight Shine into Their Hearts
Hebrews 4:12-13, Philippians 4:7, Romans 12:2, 1 John 2:15-17, 1 Chronicles 28:9, Ephesians 5:26-27, 2 Corinthians 3:18

9. Shining Stars Think What God Thinks
1 Corinthians 2:10-16, Ephesians 1:17-18, Ephesians 4:17-24, 2 Corinthians 5:17, Colossians 3:10, Galatians 5:22, Philippians 4:8

10. Shining Stars Do What God Does
Galatians 5:22, John 5:19, James 1:22-25, James 2:14-17, Ephesians 2:10, Philippians 2:13, Philippians 1:11

11. Shining Stars Are Salty
Matthew 5:15-16, Philippians 2:15-16, Matthew 28:18-20, Mark 16:20, John 14:12-14, Revelation 12:9, Matthew 16:23

12. Shining Stars Are Leaders
Mark 10:13-16, 1 Timothy 1:7, 2 Timothy 3:14-15, Matthew 21:15-16, Psalm 8:2, Matthew 18:2-4

1. Shining Stars See the Big Picture

We all want to live a good life and we all want to be good people. It doesn't always work out that way because humans aren't perfect. But that's okay – God, who created the world and created you and me, is the One who knows the best way to live and He is here to help us! That's because God understands *everything* – He sees the big picture (He *made* the big picture) and when we get to know God, He helps us see the big picture too.

God didn't create the universe and then stand back and watch us from a distance. He is with us *now* and He knows everything about us – He knows you better than you know yourself! He wants you to know Him too so that you can have a *relationship* with Him. As you know Him better and better each day, you will see God's big picture of life on this earth. You will understand that there is nothing more amazing than God and there is nothing more perfect than his way. You will become a Shining Star in God's world!

When stars shine they give a lot of light. The sun is not the biggest star in space, but it is the closest one to the earth even though it's 93 million miles away! If you could travel to the sun in your car, going as fast you do on a highway, it would take you 150 years to get there! Even though it's so far away, the sun is bright enough to light up our earth and the other planets in our solar system. With the sun's light we can see our world, we can learn more about it, enjoy it more, and use things in it to help us live. Think of yourself as a Shining Star, just like the sun. As Shining Stars, we shine God's light on the earth so people can see what God is like and they can understand his best way.

The Bible says, *Among these people you shine like stars in the world because you hold on to the word of life* (Philippians 2:15-16 CEB). We provide light for people who don't know God, and even for people who do! God is full of *wisdom* (He understands everything) and full of *every good thing*. When we get to know God He gives us his wisdom so that we actually become more like Him! He fills our lives with his light until we shine, and everyone around us can see his wisdom and his goodness shining through. But if God is so amazing, how can we possibly get to know Him? Sometimes we feel like God is as far away from us as the sun is! In fact, He is much closer than that, and He *wants* you to get to know Him. This book shows you how!

★ ★ ★ ★ ★

"God, You created this whole universe and You created me in it. You know everything there is to know, and You are everything that is good. I have so much to learn about You and I want to start today. I know that You will help me to understand the way You are, and the best way we can live here on the earth. I want to become more like You so your light shines through me – help me to be a Shining Star!"

God is the one who used his power and made the earth. He used his wisdom and built the world. With his understanding He stretched the sky over the earth. Jeremiah 10:12

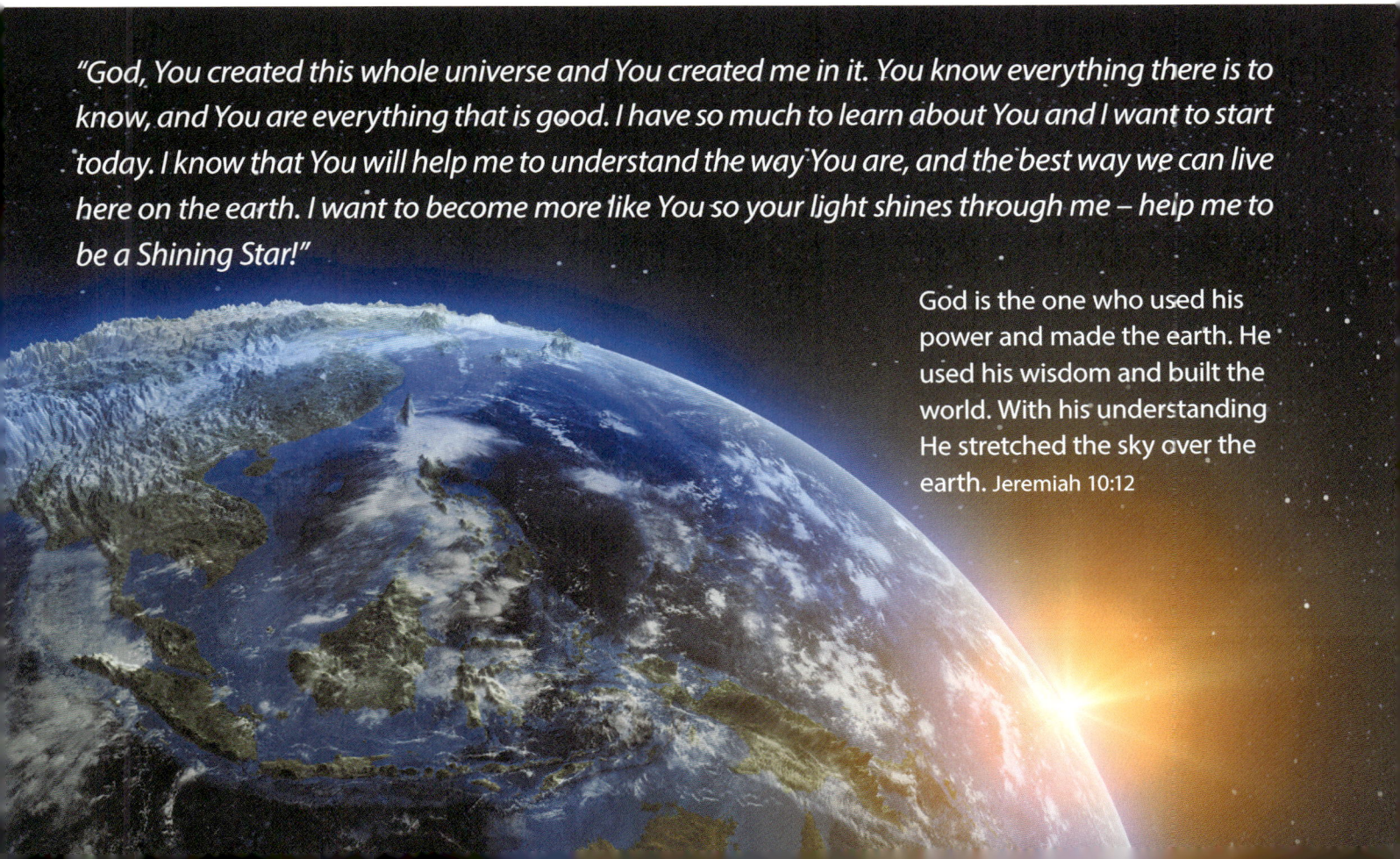

2. Shining Stars Focus on God, Not on Rules

Do you sometimes try really hard to be a good person? Maybe you try to be helpful to your parents, to be a good friend, and to finish your homework. You might want to be an extra nice person because you think Christians are supposed to be that way.

Sometimes we make rules for ourselves to help us be good people. We tell ourselves, 'I need to smile more often' or 'I need to do one thing to help somebody each day.' On top of that, we have rules from the government like crossing the street at the right time and not stealing other people's things. Our parents and teachers give us rules too. How many rules can one person follow?

The Israelites (God's special nation before Jesus came) had a *lot* of rules. God put the rules there to help them live good lives because He knew what was best for them. But then He sent his Son Jesus to the earth to show people an *even better* way. Jesus said, 'God told you not to kill someone, but I am telling you that even if you say something mean to someone, that is just as bad.' The people thought that was too hard. They said, 'What you are telling us to do is impossible!' Jesus agreed. 'You're right, it is impossible for you to keep all these rules, but with God you can live a good life.'

What that means is, the only way to live the good life you want is to live with God. God came to the earth as a human being to show people how to do this. But He also died as a human being so people wouldn't need to worry about keeping rules anymore, but would focus on getting to know God. When we have a relationship with God we become more like Him and we can't help but live a different kind of life – we live God's *best way*.

The Bible writers talked a lot about something called *grace*. Grace is doing something good for someone even if they don't deserve it. God is *all about* grace. He sent his Son Jesus to die for all of the people in the world so that it doesn't matter what we *do*! Whether we think we're doing good things or bad things, God doesn't look at those things. We don't need to try to please God! Think about your mom or your dad, or maybe someone else who takes care of you. Do they love you because of the things you do? No, they love you because you are you! God is like that even more. He loves us exactly as we are and He just wants us to get to know Him better.

So instead of trying so hard to be good, let's just get to know God and enjoy being with Him.

★ ★ ★ ★ ★

"God, I have tried to be a good person by following rules and it doesn't work very well, or at least, not for very long. Thank you for your grace. Jesus died for people because You loved us, not because we kept all the rules. Thank-you that You love me no matter what I do, and that all You want is for me to know You better."

He saved us because of his [grace], not because of any good things we did. Titus 3:5

3. Shining Stars Think God is Amazing

Have you ever stopped to think about who God is? He created the universe, He knows everything from the beginning to the end of time, He is everywhere at the same time, He is love, He is goodness, He is perfect. It's hard for our minds to totally grasp how amazing God is, and that's okay because we have a lifetime to learn more about Him and get to know Him.

There's a quick way to remind ourselves, though, of all of the awesome ways God is so great – we can find it in the Bible! The Bible is a book written by people who knew God really well. Here's what they had to say about Him:

★ God created the sky and the earth. (Genesis 1:1)
★ Every word that God speaks is true. (Proverbs 30:5)
★ The Lord God says… "I am the One who is, who always was, and who is coming. I am the All-Powerful." (Revelation 1:8)
★ God's word is alive and working. (Hebrews 4:12)
★ The Lord is a kind and merciful God. He is slow to become angry. He is full of great love. He can be trusted. (Exodus 34:6)
★ Love comes from God. God is love. (1 John 4:7,8)
★ God is light, and in Him there is no darkness. (1 John 1:5)
★ [God said] "I am…the first and the last, the beginning and the end." (Revelation 22:12)
★ God lives forever. He is your place of safety. His power continues forever! He is protecting you. (Deuteronomy 33:27)
★ You [God] formed the way I think and feel. You put me together in my mother's womb. I praise You because You made me in such a wonderful way. (Psalm 139: 13-14)

- ★ The Lord is good and merciful; our God is so kind. (Psalm 116:5)
- ★ The Lord takes care of helpless people. (Psalm 116:6)
- ★ [Jesus said] "I leave you peace. It is my own peace I give you. I give you peace in a different way than the world does. So don't be troubled. Don't be afraid." (John 14:27)
- ★ The fruit that [God] produces in a person's life is love, joy, peace, patience, kindness, goodness, faithfulness, gentleness, and self-control. (Galatians 5:22-23)

This is our God. This is the One who created us and wants to help us understand who He is and how to live his awesome way – how to be Shining Stars in this wonderful world He made for us to live in!

★ ★ ★ ★ ★

"God, I am so impressed with how amazing You are. You are the God of the universe, and even though I feel so small in this huge universe, I know I am important to You because You say that I am. I want to learn more about You and get to know You better."

Come, let us bow down and worship Him! Let us kneel before the Lord who made us. He is our God, and we are the people He cares for. Psalm 95:6-7

4. Shining Stars Know Why Jesus Lived, Died, and Lived Again

The Bible explains God in three ways: a Father, a Son, and a Spirit. It is hard to understand, even for adults, how God is three beings at the same time. God the Father, the Creator of the universe, is the easiest to understand. Most of the verses in Chapter 3 talk about Him. We call Him the *Father* because He has a *Son*, Jesus. This chapter is about Jesus. (The next chapter will be about the Spirit.)

God put himself inside a human being named Jesus more than 2,000 years ago to show us how we can have a *relationship* with God and live his best way. The Bible calls Jesus God's *Son*, but it also calls Him *God* because He had God living inside Him. Jesus did some incredible things: He healed people who were sick, turned a storm into calm weather, and even made people come alive again after they died! But He also loved people and cared about them - He allowed God's love to flow through Him to other people. He talked with God all the time and He saw life the way God sees it. He knew what to do every day, every moment, to live God's way.

Jesus did something else that was very important: He died. Some people didn't like Jesus because He could see into their hearts and He knew that even though they said they loved God, really they didn't. These people arranged to have Jesus killed by nailing Him to a cross (that was one of the ways they used to punish criminals – people who had done very bad things). Jesus could have just left the earth without dying because He was God. But God's plan was that He would die as a human being (as Jesus). He loved people so much that He wanted to take away everything that was getting in the way for them to *really* know Him and be close to Him.

In Chapter 2 we talked about rules. People sometimes break rules, right? When the Israelites broke a rule they needed to bring a *sacrifice* to God – often an animal would need to die so the person who broke the rule wouldn't be punished. Jesus was the *last sacrifice for all of the rule-breaking* that people would ever do! That means we don't need to think about rules - we are free to think about God, how much He loves us, and how awesome He is.

But Jesus didn't stay dead: after three days, He came alive again! With God inside Him, He was even more powerful than death. After coming alive again Jesus told his followers, 'God has given me power over everything in heaven and on earth. Teach people the things I have taught you. I will be with you always.' If Jesus is with us always, we have his power with us always too!

★ ★ ★ ★ ★

God sent his Son into the world. He did not send Him to judge the world guilty, but to save the world through Him. John 3:17

"God, thank-you for sending Jesus to show us how to live with You every day. It's sad that He had to die but I know He did something very important: He helped us get closer to You without having to follow all those rules. Thank-you that Jesus came alive again and that He has power over everything. Help me to remember that Jesus is always with me and that his power is with me too!"

5. Shining Stars Listen to God's Spirit

A little while after Jesus came alive again He told his followers it was time for Him to leave the earth to be with God the Father. His followers were sad and worried that they might forget all of the things He taught them. But Jesus told them not to worry because He would send them his Spirit – God's Spirit – to remind them and to teach them more about God. The Bible says God's Spirit (sometimes called the Holy Spirit) is like an invisible helper for everyone who believes in Jesus. It also says the Spirit is God! Can you believe that God Himself is always right beside you in the form of his Spirit?

But how do we really know He's there? We cannot see the Spirit with our eyes, we cannot hear Him with our ears, and we cannot touch Him. Here's how we know: He gives us thoughts and ideas, and even a desire to do things.

How do we know which thoughts are from God's Spirit? Here's an example that might help you understand. Let's say you have a cousin who you've never met because she lives far away. One day she calls you on the phone and you have no idea who it is - you don't recognize her voice! But the next time she calls, you might remember the sound of her voice. Let's say she calls every day – after a few days you recognize her as soon as she says 'Hello'!

It's the same with God's Spirit. If you listen every day, you will begin to know what the Spirit's 'voice' sounds like. Maybe you're starting to listen today! Try this: find a quiet place and ask God to speak to you through his Spirit. All you have to do is sit quietly. You might notice many different thoughts going through your mind. This is normal because our minds are always very busy, but we can learn to ignore all of those thoughts and wait for a special thought from God. God's thoughts are always wise and good, and never go against anything in the Bible. And here's the exciting part: God's Spirit will say something just for you because God knows exactly what you need to hear each day!

Another way of listening to God is by reading what other people have written about Him. The *Bible* is a book that has many stories and poems written about God and about Jesus. All of the people who wrote parts of the Bible knew God very well. God can speak to us through the Bible even today! The things God says is called his 'Word'. The Spirit speaks God's Word to us as we read the Bible and as we listen for his thoughts of truth in our minds. Try listening to what the Spirit is saying to you by reading a little bit of the Bible each day.

★ ★ ★ ★ ★

"I know your Holy Spirit is with me all the time, and gives me wisdom to understand things the way You understand them. God, help me to hear what You are saying to me in my thoughts when I spend quiet time with You, and when I read the Bible."

Your Word [things God says] is like a lamp that guides my steps, a light that shows the path I should take. Psalm 119:105

6. Shining Stars Talk With God

Talking with God is what Christians call *prayer*. Sometimes we think prayer is just asking God to do things for us, but it's so much more! Prayer is having a conversation with God – it's talking *with* Him, not only *to* Him. If we want to have a good conversation with someone, we need to do some of the talking *and* some of the listening.

But what can you talk with God about, since He already knows everything? It doesn't matter - God wants to have a *relationship* with you and that means you can talk with Him about anything that is going on in your life, in other people's lives, in your city, in your country, in the world. You can talk with Him about things you hear, things you read - anything that is on your mind. God cares about everything that is going on in your life and in other people's lives. When we talk about these things with Him and ask Him to help us understand the way He understands, He shows us what his *will* is – this is the perfect and right thing that should happen in every situation: God's best way. And this is the thing we can ask for when we pray, and know God wants it too! The Bible says when we ask for God's best way, it will happen.

Did you know that Jesus prayed a lot? He prayed early in the morning, He prayed in the middle of the day, and sometimes He prayed all night long! Jesus was God but He was also human, and just like us, He went through many things each day and needed to make sure his *will* (what He wanted) was the same as God's will (God's best way). If Jesus spent lots of time talking with God, it's probably a good idea for us too!

Spending time with God by yourself every day can help you get to know God better. Choose a place where there is nothing that will distract you from your conversation with God and give it a try. Remember to talk and to listen! (I like to talk out loud when I spend my time with God each day - it helps me concentrate.)

Jesus spent a lot of time with God this way, but He also talked with God quietly in his mind *all day long*, wherever He was. He only said to people what He heard God saying to his thoughts, and He only did what He knew was God's perfect way (God's *will*). We can talk with God this way too, all day long! When Jesus was on the earth, people asked Him how to pray. Here's what He said (Christians call this 'The Lord's Prayer'):

★ ★ ★ ★ ★

"God, You are awesome. Let me tell You about some of the things I am thinking about so I can know what your will is - that's the way I want things to happen here on earth too. Thank-you that we don't need to worry about anything because You love us and take care of us each day. I know You forget about the things I do that are not right - I also want to forget about things other people do that I don't like. Please remind me when I am thinking too much about things that are not good. You are the King of the universe, and You are in control of everything." (from Matthew 6:9-13)

The prayer of a [person who loves God] is powerful and effective.
James 5:16 (NIV)

7. Shining Stars Thank God for Taking Care of Them

The Bible tells us that *every good thing* comes straight from God. Each of us has so many good things to thank God for. Christians call these things *blessings*. Think about some of the blessings you might have in your life: good friends, parents who know God, a nice teacher, a great school, a pet that you love, a comfortable house, even beautiful flowers and trees that God made. You can also thank God for blessings that He has given to other people. Maybe you have been asking God to help someone and He has!

Some people think that God gives bad things too. That's just because they don't know Him. God never makes people get sick and He never does things to make people sad. Bad things happen on earth because God's will (his best way) doesn't happen everywhere, all the time. When we spend time talking with God, we learn more every day about what He is *like* (his character). God's Spirit reminds us that God is good and loving and takes care of us - He never gives us bad things.

Do you know someone who always wishes he had what other people have? He never seems happy because he is always thinking about what he doesn't have. We *all* feel this way sometimes, don't we? Can you think of something someone else has that you want? But you can also think about something you are glad you have. That is called being *content*, and the Bible tells us it is better to think this way. Being thankful keeps our hearts full of joy and reminds us to be content with what we have. This is a healthy way to live, and God wants us to live happy, healthy lives.

God has so many great things for us to learn and do during our time here on the earth. These are 100 times better than the things we wish we had! When Jesus was on the earth,

He told people not to worry about what they would eat, or the clothes they would wear, or how they would stay healthy. Jesus said that God takes care of flowers, so of course He cares even more about us! He knows everything we need before we even ask. He said, 'You don't need to worry about these things because God knows you need them and He wants to give them to you. Instead, think about God's *will*, his best way in everything that happens. Then you will really see how God takes care of you!' When we let go of the things that we are worried about and thank God that He takes care of us, He gives us his *peace*. Peace is having a relaxed mind because we're not worried about anything. God's peace is an awesome thing!

★ ★ ★ ★ ★

"God, I want to be content with what I have. I know that You are taking care of everything in my life because You want the very best for me. Thank you for all of the good things You have given to me and to other people. There are so many things I can thank You for – here are just a few… [think of some things to thank God for and say them out loud]. I don't want to think about what I want, I want to think about your best way all the time, wherever I am."

Everything good comes from God. Every perfect gift is from Him. These good gifts come down from the Father who made all the lights in the sky. James 1:17

8. Shining Stars Let God's Flashlight Shine into Their Hearts

When we listen to God's Spirit, He tells us many things. Everything He says is true and helps us to understand the way things really are. Sometimes the Holy Spirit helps us to see deep inside our own thoughts, into what we *really* want. It's like He shines a flashlight into the corners of our heart so we can see what's hiding there. Of course, God already knows everything we're thinking but sometimes *we* don't notice all of our thoughts. The flashlight of the Holy Spirit helps us see what's there so we can bring it in line with God's best way.

We know that living for God is not about following rules. God gives us his Spirit for free because of his grace - we don't need to be good to receive it. But God helps us to be *pure* as we get to know Him more. A *pure* heart is one that only wants God's best way – his will. Jesus had pure *motives*. Motives are the deep-down thoughts we have that make us do what we do. They are the things we *really want*. Everything you do starts with a motive. For example, you might clean your room because your parents said you can play a computer game when you're done. What you *really want* is to play a computer game – that's your motive for cleaning your room.

Sometimes our motives are opposite to God's best way. John, a man who was very close to Jesus when He was on the earth, told people what these opposite motives usually are: wanting things that we think will make us happy, and wanting other people to think we're great. Have you ever wanted those things? Everyone has, and that's okay because God cleans our hearts every day as we talk with Him so that our motives move in line with God's will.

Paul was a man who wrote lots of letters to churches a long time ago to help them learn more about Jesus and God's best way. Many of these letters are in the Bible so *we* can read them too. In one of his letters, Paul says that our thoughts and our motives will be completely changed into God's best way if we let the Holy Spirit change them. No problem, right? Well, maybe not. It doesn't always feel nice when the Spirit shows us our motives – what if the Spirit shows you that you really want people to think you're great? At first you might feel bad, but you don't need to! The Spirit reminds us that God made us as we are and He thinks we're great. It doesn't matter, then, what anyone else thinks, does it? God knows that changing our motives sometimes takes time. As we let God's Spirit shine his flashlight into the corners of our hearts, He changes us every day to become more and more like Him.

★ ★ ★ ★ ★

"God, some of the things I want are all about making me happy or making other people think I'm great. I want my motives to be in line with your best way, and when I talk with You, I let You shine your flashlight into my heart to show me what my motives are. You see everything people think and You always want what is best for us. I want to become more like You every day – pure and full of goodness just like Jesus."

God, create a pure heart in me and make my spirit strong again.

Psalm 51:10

9. Shining Stars Think What God Thinks

When we talk with God every day, telling Him about the things that are on our minds and listening to the Spirit help us understand God's best way for them, after a little while we actually begin to *think* like Jesus thinks! If we let Him, God will make us to be more like Him, to think the way He thinks. In the Bible, Paul said, 'Who can know what God is thinking? We can because the Holy Spirit tells us!' We know the Spirit is with us always, speaking to us through our thoughts and helping us to understand God's truth about everything. The Bible also says that as we get to know God better and learn about his best way, He changes us to become like new people – we become like Jesus and that means we can think the same things that Jesus thinks.

So, what does Jesus think about? In Chapter 3 we talked about how amazing God is. Remember that God (Jesus) is love, He is goodness, and the things that come from God are love, joy, peace, patience, kindness, goodness, faithfulness, gentleness, and self-control. God's thoughts are always on these things. The Bible calls them the fruit of the Spirit, and we'll talk more about them in the next chapter.

Paul tells us about some of the other things that God thinks about, and encourages us to let his Spirit remind us to think about them too: whatever is true, respectful, pure and good. Paul also tells us that God's thoughts about people are always good because He loves them. When God gives us his thoughts, we will always see the good in other people, and we will always want the very best for them – God's best way!

You choose which thoughts to think about everything that happens in your life. If you are talking with God (remember, that's talking and listening!) and getting to know Him better, his Spirit will give you his thoughts - what *Jesus* thinks - about everything that happens in your life. For example, let's say there's a kid at school who acts like a bully. He's mean and not many kids like him. What do *you* think about him? Do you think, 'I don't like him either and I wish he would leave our school'? That's a normal way to think, but God's thoughts are often different than our thoughts. If we listen to his Spirit, He helps us understand *why* people do what they do, and He helps us to see the good things about them. His thoughts about people are always good because He loves each person He made as much as He loves you. When you ask God what *He* thinks about someone, his Spirit will fill your heart with God's love for that person. Then you will understand how to pray for him, and even how to help him!

★ ★ ★ ★ ★

"It's exciting, God, to know that your Spirit gives us your thoughts when we listen. You always think about what is good, true, and respectful of other people. My own thoughts aren't always about those things, but I thank You that You change us to be like You as we learn more about You every day. You help us to understand your best way about everything that happens in life."

…let God change you inside with a new way of thinking. Then you will be able to understand and accept what God wants for you. You will be able to know what is good and pleasing to Him and what is perfect. Romans 12:2

10. Shining Stars Do What God Does

You might have heard of the fruit of the Spirit: love, joy, peace, patience, kindness, goodness, faithfulness, gentleness, and self-control. These are the things your life will be full of when you listen to God's Spirit and let God change the way you think to be more like how He thinks. When you think like God thinks, you will also *do* what God *does* and the 'fruit' that comes from your life will be the fruit of the Spirit!

To help us understand this better let's choose a fruit we know, like grapes. If you want some grapes you need to pick them from a grapevine or buy them from someone who has picked them from a grapevine. You can't make grapes on your own - only grapevines can make grapes. It's the same with the fruit of the Spirit. You can't *make* love, joy, peace, patience, kindness, goodness, faithfulness, gentleness, and self-control on your own, at least not for very long. They are not rules to follow, they are fruit that come from the 'grapevine' of God. God is all about these things - they describe exactly who God *is*.

The Holy Spirit is like the food that the grapevine takes from the soil, and the sun, and the rain, and works through the branches to make grapes. In the same way, God's wisdom from his Spirit flows into us and through us, and out of us too – it keeps flowing! It's a good thing grapevines don't just *think* about growing grapes, but they actually *do* it. Otherwise we wouldn't have any grapes to enjoy! When Jesus was on the earth, He told people that He not only listened to what God said - He also *did* what He knew God would do wherever He was, every day!

Let's say on the playground at school you see a new kid in your class playing by himself. If you are listening to the Spirit in that moment, He would tell you how much God loves that kid and fill your heart with God's love for him too. And you might suddenly get a thought: that kid needs someone to go over and be his friend! Is that thought good and pure, and full of love? Then it is from God – the Spirit has just given you a thought Jesus would think! So what do you do? Do you pray and ask God to send someone so that his will can be done in this moment? No, you *do* it because you're right there. This is how God's will happens through you!

In the Bible, Paul tells us that long before we were born God planned many good things for us to do during our time on this earth. The things you say and do are the fruit that comes out of you, the branch. If we stay connected to the vine of Jesus, his Spirit produces love, joy, and peace inside of us and we can't help but let it flow over into what we say and do!

★ ★ ★ ★ ★

"God, when I talk with You about things, You tell me your best way for them – your will. Thank-you for giving me Your thoughts so I can know your will and do your will. I want the fruit of the Spirit to grow inside me and come out of me just like grapes on a grapevine. I will stay connected to You by talking with You every day."

I am the vine, and you are the branches. If you stay joined to Me, and I to you, you will produce plenty of fruit. But separated from Me you won't be able to do anything. John 15:5

11. Shining Stars Are Salty

Did you know Jesus said his followers are like *salt*? Think about a bowl of soup that tastes plain. When you add just a *bit* of salt and stir it around, the whole bowl of soup tastes great! So how are we like salt? We can help people around us learn more about God and his best way just by being who we are! Jesus was very salty. The Bible has a lot of stories where huge crowds of people came to find Jesus so they could be with Him all day. When they tasted just a bit of God's truth that Jesus offered, it made them feel alive!

Jesus told his followers, 'You are a light that shines for the world to see.' Paul said that people who know Jesus are like stars in the sky, holding out God's truth for everyone in the world to see and to have (that's why this book is called Shining Stars!). Did you know that God's truth and love *in* you, from the Holy Spirit, is what everyone around you needs? You are the salt that can help them live with God's love, joy, and peace in their hearts too, just by being around them!

There's one more thing we need to remember about being salt on the earth: nobody can take away our saltiness! The devil (Satan) was the angel who turned against God before people were created. He wanted to be God himself, so God kicked him out of heaven and Satan convinced some of the other angels to go with him (those are the demons). Now they are on the earth trying to turn people away from God. They can speak to people's thoughts just like the Holy Spirit can, but they just tell lies and hope people will believe them. Jesus gave us power over the devil so we don't need to be afraid, and we don't need to let him do what he wants! It is never God's will that the devil gets his way. When we speak something or do something to make God's will happen, the devil has no power to stop us. The only way we can become less salty is if we stop letting the Holy Spirit fill us with saltiness.

Saltiness means being like Jesus on the earth and doing the things He did. What about the *miracles* He did, like making sick people get well and even making people who had died come alive again? Yes, we can do those things too! God gave Jesus power over *everything* on the earth and Jesus gave that power to his followers – that's us! But doing miracles wasn't the main thing Jesus came to do. What He *really* wanted was to help people taste God's love, God's joy, God's peace, and all of the other fruit of the Spirit, by tasting Him. So, what do you taste like?

★ ★ ★ ★ ★

"God, I want to be salty so that when people are with me they can taste your saltiness: all the good things that You are. I need to stay connected to You like a branch on a tree so that the life of your Spirit comes into me and out of me to other people. I don't want to lose my saltiness, because then when people are with me they will only taste me and not You. You are what everyone needs."

"You [people who know God] are the salt of the earth…you are the light that shines for the world to see." Matthew 5:13a,14

12. Shining Stars Are Leaders

Have you ever thought that *really* getting to know God is something you start doing when you're an adult? Maybe you've thought that for now you'll keep going to Sunday school and learning a little bit about God but when you're older, that's when you'll really start to have a relationship with Him?

Now that you've read almost all of this book, I hope you know that your awesome life with God is happening *right now*! As you talk with God and listen to Him during quiet times and all day long, you will get to know what He is really like – you will know his *character*. You will see more and more how perfect and amazing He is, and how God's way is the best way for everything in your life and the lives of people around you.

One day when Jesus was speaking to a large crowd about who God is, people brought their children to Him so He could pray for them. His followers told the people, 'Don't bother Jesus with your children - it's more important for Him to talk to the adults.' But Jesus said that's not true. 'Bring the children to Me,' He said, 'because the Kingdom of God is for people like them!' When the Bible talks about the *Kingdom of God*, it means God's best way – his will. The Kingdom of God is wherever God's will is happening. That means kids make God's will happen! Jesus told people that they need to become like children if they want to be in God's Kingdom – they need to be humble and trust Him like children do!

In the Bible, Paul said that it doesn't matter how young you are, you can set an example in God's Kingdom. He said, 'Don't let anyone look down on you because you are young, but set an example for God's people in the way you talk, the way you live, how much you love people, the faith you have in God, and in how your good life shows respect for God.'

Setting an example means being a leader. It means showing other people what it looks like to know and love God. You can even be an example for adults! You don't need to wait until you're older to be a leader.

Every day when you fill yourself up with God's Word of life (his shining light) by talking with Him and learning more and more about how incredible and good He is, his light flows through you to everyone around you – people can see God in you! That's what being a leader is!

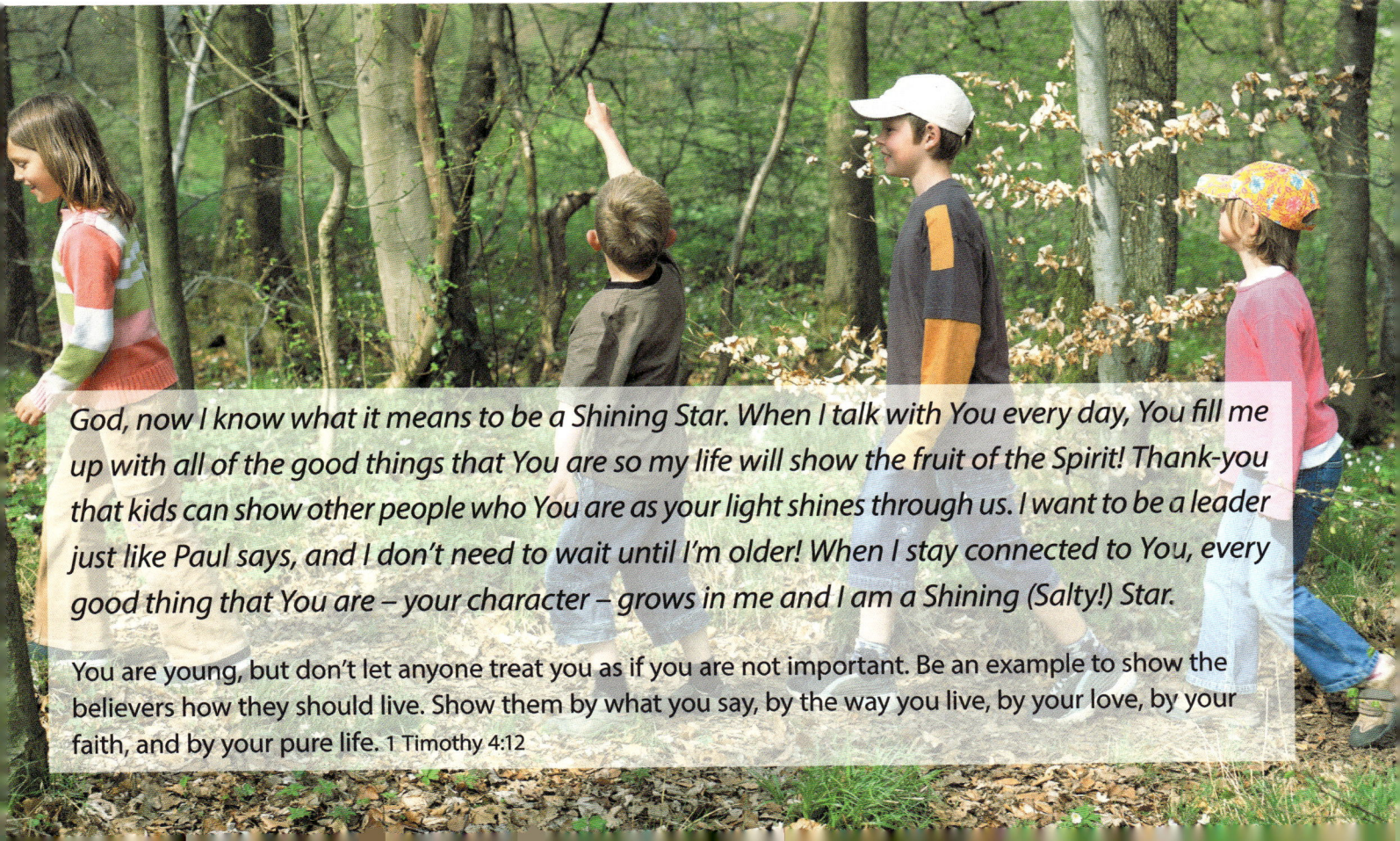

★ ★ ★ ★ ★

God, now I know what it means to be a Shining Star. When I talk with You every day, You fill me up with all of the good things that You are so my life will show the fruit of the Spirit! Thank-you that kids can show other people who You are as your light shines through us. I want to be a leader just like Paul says, and I don't need to wait until I'm older! When I stay connected to You, every good thing that You are – your character – grows in me and I am a Shining (Salty!) Star.

You are young, but don't let anyone treat you as if you are not important. Be an example to show the believers how they should live. Show them by what you say, by the way you live, by your love, by your faith, and by your pure life. 1 Timothy 4:12

Time to Start Shining!

God's Shining Stars know that God is amazing and that his way is the best way. They know that Jesus made it possible for us to know God, to know what He thinks, and to have his power to do the things Jesus did when He was on the earth. Each day, we talk with God and listen to Him through his Holy Spirit, and we learn more about Him by reading the Bible too. We let God shine the flashlight of the Spirit into every corner of our heart so we can become more like Him.

Shining Stars don't need to worry about anything because they know God loves them and takes care of them. That means they can focus on knowing Him, loving Him, and making his best way happen in their lives and other people's lives too. They are salty and make life taste better for people around them. They are bright, and shine God's light for people around them. They are like branches on God's grapevine, connected to God's wisdom and showing people around them the fruit of the Spirit – love, joy, peace, patience, kindness, goodness, faithfulness, gentleness, and self-control.

Let's stay connected to God and be his Shining Stars today, tomorrow, the next day, and grow brighter and brighter every day!

You are the light that shines for the world to see…Live so that they will see the good things you do and praise your Father in heaven. Matthew 5:14, 16

CPSIA information can be obtained
at www.ICGtesting.com
Printed in the USA
402629LV00003B/6